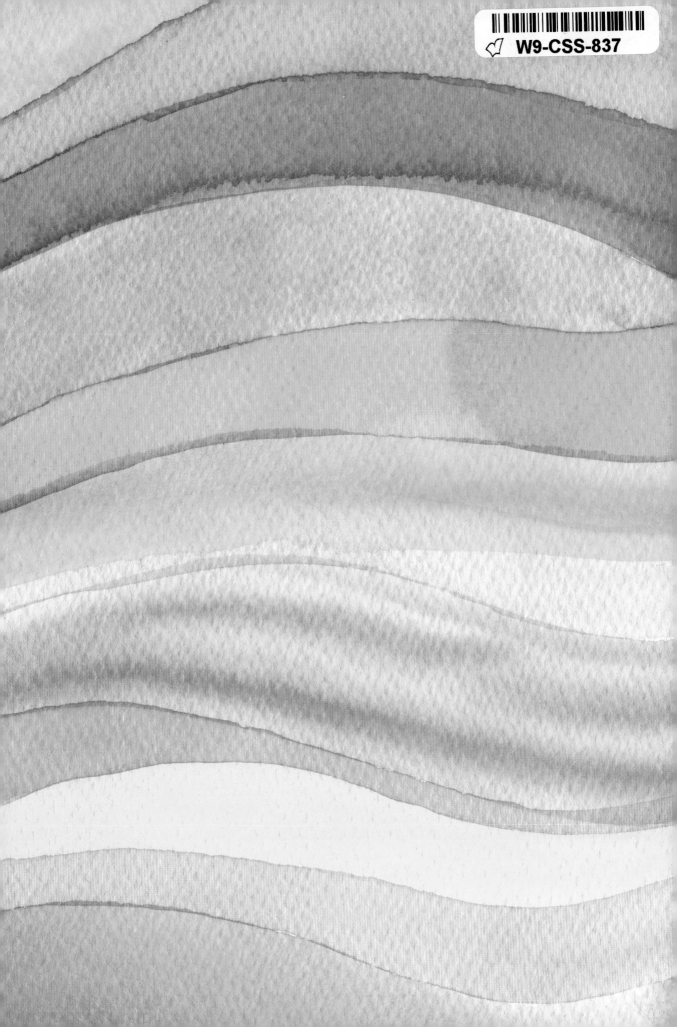

No matter the day, no matter the month, no matter the year, there's always something to celebrate!

Some holidays are fixed on a certain date (*National Cereal Day*, March 7), and some change year to year (*Pancake Day*). But whenever they happen (*Look Alike Day*, April 20), and why ever they happen (*Hug a Greeting Card Writer Day*), a poem is always a great way to start the festivities.

There are days honoring almost everything. Some drop off our calendar, and new ones are added every year. Have a great idea? Do some research, gather some like-minded supporters, get out a pencil and paper, and off you go!

# KooKY CRUmbS

## Poems in Praise of Dizzy Days

*To Beth, Matt, and Leigh Ann—my kooky kids—*
*Love, Dad*
**J.P.L.**

*For all of my teachers and friends from beginning to middle,*
*especially Tim Carothers and Susan Eaddy*
**Mary Uhles**

Kane Miller, A Division of EDC Publishing

Text copyright © J. Patrick Lewis 2016
Illustrations copyright © Mary Uhles 2016

For information contact:
Kane Miller, A Division of EDC Publishing
PO Box 470663
Tulsa, OK 74147-0663

**www.kanemiller.com**
**www.edcpub.com**
**www.usbornebooksandmore.com**

Library of Congress Control Number: 2015938806

Manufactured by Regent Publishing Services, Hong Kong
Printed March 2016 in ShenZhen, Guangdong, China

ISBN: 978-1-61067-371-6

2 3 4 5 6 7 8 9 10

# KOOKY CRUMBS

## Poems in Praise of Dizzy Days

Written by J. Patrick Lewis

Illustrated by Mary Uhles

**Kane Miller**

A DIVISION OF EDC PUBLISHING

# The Names of Queen Nefertiti

Queen Nefertiti, for all her fame,
Could not decide on the perfect name.

Lady of Grace had a nose like a sparrow,
Eyes like rubies, and a hubby like a pharaoh.

Lady of Egypt (Upper and Lower)
Rode wherever peasants would row her.

Great of Praises stayed so slim
Working out in a fitness gym.

Sweet of Love, Ruler of the Nile,
Fair of Face (Is that a smile?),

Lady of Two Lands aristocrat,
Where can I get a hat like that?

National
Hat Day

# Weather Is for the Verbs

Wind whines,
Fog blinds,
Rain thrums,
Hail drums,
Ice crumbs,
Sleet whips,
Snow grips,
Frost nips—
Weather persons,
"Winter worsens."
Cloud looms,
Lightning blooms,
Thunder booms,
Cold dies,
Spring tries,
Breeze creaks,
Heat seeks
August peaks—
Weather splendor,
Summer ender!

# A Bicycle Built for Ten

On a bicycle built for ten—
Be it boys and girls, women or men—
   You must pedal and pedal
    And pedal and pedal,
And then you must pedal again.

But here is the odd thing: At last,
No matter the records surpassed,
   Though you pedal and pedal
    And pedal and pedal,
You cannot go ten times as fast.

Inventors'
Day

# FINGER PLAY

Teenagers can talk with a finger,
Teenagers can shout with a thumb
Because fingertip-typing whole sentences
Proves you must be pretty dumb.

Tap rapid-fire on your cell phone
Memos misspelled from the start
Because spelling without enough letters
Proves you must be pretty smart.

A telephone hangs in the kitchen
Collecting dust, so I am told,
Because using the phone is so yesterday
And proves you must be pretty old.

World Telecommunications Day

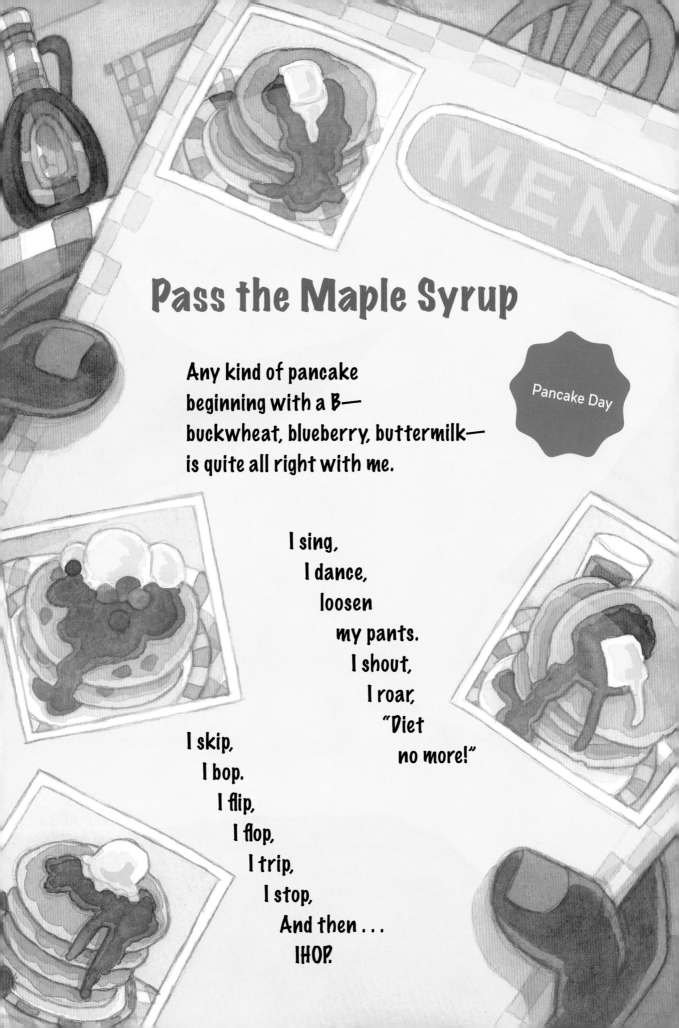

# Pass the Maple Syrup

Pancake Day

Any kind of pancake
beginning with a B—
buckwheat, blueberry, buttermilk—
is quite all right with me.

I sing,
I dance,
loosen
my pants.
I shout,
I roar,
"Diet
no more!"

I skip,
I bop.
I flip,
I flop,
I trip,
I stop,
And then . . .
IHOP.

# Grape-Nuts

I eat Grape-Nuts with raisins—
One of my breakfast habits—
But I make sure I don't confuse
My raisins with the rabbit's.

National
Cereal Day

World
Math Day

## First Ever Idea for Arithmetic

Add two numbers together,
And you'll get sumthing else.

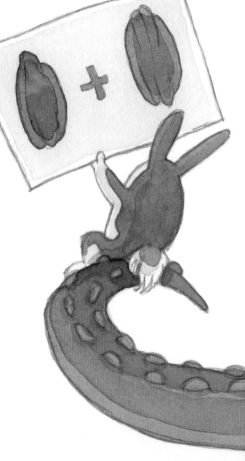

# Disconnected

I was calling my Aunt Nina
When I heard from Argentina
That she'd met a crocodile . . .
So I took her off speed dial.

# Zipper-up Zack

Zipper-up Zack
Wore zippers galore.
He had more zippers
Than a fabric store.
He zipped his arms,
His legs and feet,
He zipped himself
To the toilet seat.
He zipped his toes,
His stomach and hips,
His ears, nose, neck,
His tongue and lips.
He zipped his eyes,
Eyebrows, eyelids.
He zippered his wife,
Zipped up his kids!
Then Zipper-up Zack . . .

*UNZIPPERED. Hooray!*
November 16th
Is Button Day.

# The Speedy Floor Lamp

My speed has astonished the captains of science.
    My records? Too many to name.
I'm as fast as your everyday household appliance,
    I even put sofas to shame.

I leave flower pots in the shade I'm so cunning,
    I move so much faster than chairs.
Don't tell me . . . the washer and dryer are running?
    I'll easily beat them downstairs.

Homeowners will challenge me, "Can you out-hurdle
    A hat in a forty-yard sprint?"
"Have you heard," I'll reply, "of the hare and the turtle?"
    My answer is not fit to print.

Let me put in a plug: Table, there's no denying
    That floor lamps can never be beat.
Must I say it again? I'm electrifying!
    Besides I am light on my feet.

Change a
LIght Day

# The Impossibles

You cannot catch Sir Shadow—
He's such a clever chap!
But when it's dark, he catches *you*
And dozes in your lap.

You cannot climb a rainbow
Unless the winds agree
To blow in one direction—north—
Toward Curiosity.

You cannot seed a garden
With wheelbarrows of dreams—
Unless you first plant wishes
How cucumbersome it seems.

You cannot drink the ocean;
But if you drink the sea,
It takes you once around the shore—
And twice eternity.

Make Your
Dream Come
True Day

# Uncle Bertie

At summer camp
A tanning lamp
Sun-blasted Uncle Bertie,
And that explains
His spider veins
From seventeen to thirty.

A facial cream—
"Sand Blaster's Dream"—
Slapped on till he was forty
Meant Bertie's nose
Could scare scarecrows
And match a toad for warty.

Ten years went by.
He met a guy
Who told him he'd look nifty
With surgery.
It failed, and he
Looked like one hundred fifty.

Aunt Gertie said
(She bowed her head),
"Though sadness never ceases,
The wrinkles grew
For Bertie who
Found happiness in creases."

National
Sunscreen
Day

# The Longhouse of Words

You say your story's really good?
Then grab some stationery.
Inside your yellow stick of wood
You'll find the dictionary.

National
Pencil Day

# A Kite

is
a car
racing along
blue avenues of air.
It doesn't know which way
to go and doesn't care. Unruffled,
a goose flies by and honks. The car waves
back and makes a sharp U-turn down
mountains of April. Made only of
paper, balsa wood and string, it
might wind up in pieces on
the beach, but today a
five-fingered wind
swoops  in  to
give the day
a ragtag
happy
end-
in
g
g
g
g
g
g
g

# In Praise of Rolling Pins

A UFO just landed in a poison ivy patch.
Blue aliens stepped out, and instantly began to scratch.
They asked the ivy owner, Angelina Cockapoo,
*Is there a special magic that we aliens can do*
*To get rid of these bloomin' human prickles on our skin?*
She chose an ointment meant **"FOR CREATURES UGLIER THAN SIN"**
(Though she had never treated extraterrestrials before).
*Why yes*, she said, *but keep your tails and earlobes off the floor.*

She fed them each a blend of motor oil, monkey sweat,
Dead skunk perfume, shoe polish, ink, and odor de toilette.
Like bump 'em cars, the aliens came rocketing right passed her.
She beat them with a rolling pin to make the juice work faster.
Ooloomph! Delighted they were cured, they all began to cry,
Comb their teeth, bark "Thank you, human," then burp-burp, "Bye-bye."
But Angelina would not let them leave without a gift
Certificate for each: an outer spatial facial lift.

World
UFO Day

# Missing Sister

A miniature disaster
Is my blister of a sister,
Who insisted if I bossed her,
She would up and disappear.
And she did! My missing sister
Doesn't have her boss to pester,
But I thought, *What if I lost her?*
Now my mother's saying, "Dear,
She's invisible? That blister
Of a mischief-making sister?
Too bad, mister, she has missed her
Lima beans. They're getting cold."
Then she yelled, "Now listen, buster,
Find your one and only sister!"
I could no longer resist her,
So I did as I was told.

Smoke and
Mirrors Day

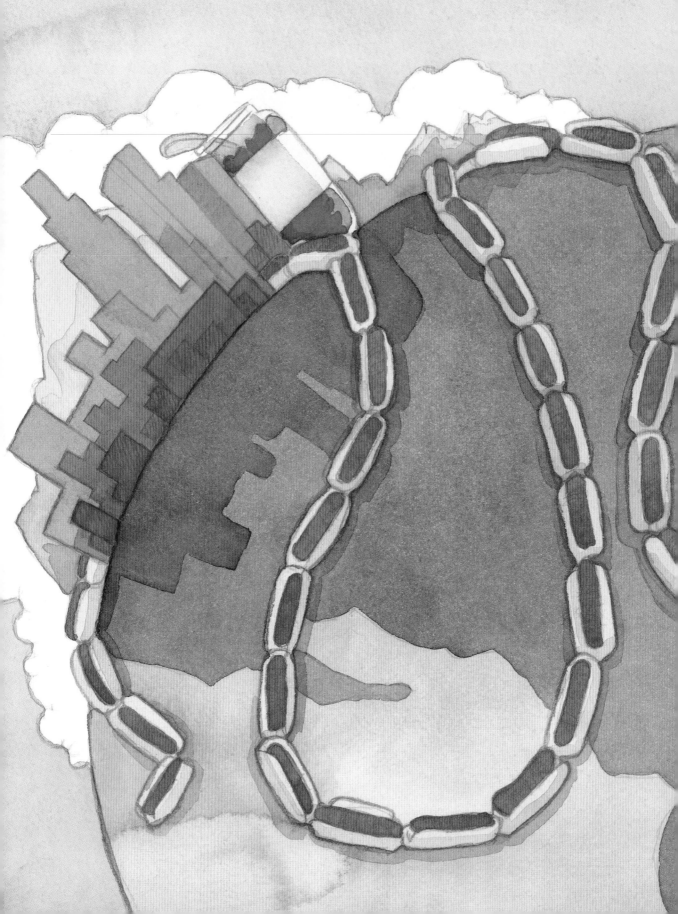

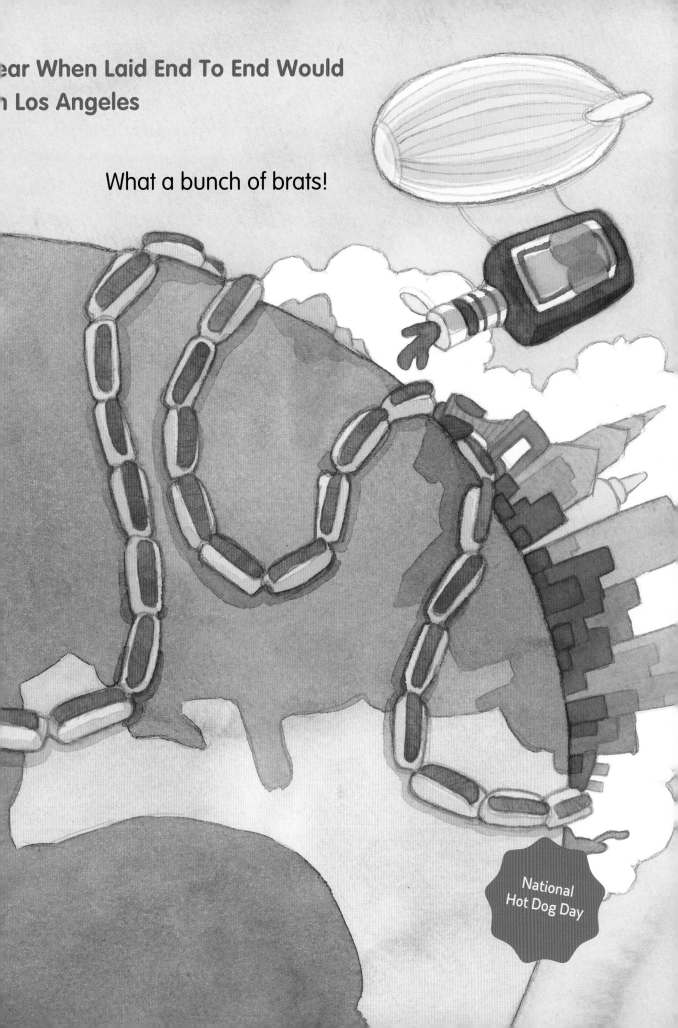

# Two Halves of a Whole

A twin is a half of a whole.
I mean, she is .5 of 1.
The other .5 is her twin.
He is the beef in the bun.

She is the bloom on the rose.
He is the moon in the sky.
She is the sauce for the goose.
He is the thumb in the pie.

He is the key to the lock.
She is the glint on the gold.
He is the star in the night.
She is the warmth in the cold.

She is the singer of songs.
He is the get-up and go.
He is the flame in the fire.
She is the afterglow.

# Food Fight

Happiness Happens Day

This is a holiday whose date
Large families ought to celebrate.
The in- and outlaws come to dine—
Linebackers in a buffet line,
And when they settle down to chow,
Imagine cattle—*Holy Cow!*
Cousin Rayford licks the bowl
Of Mama's three-bean casserole.
Uncle Bud shoots lovingly
At his wife a black-eyed pea.
My aunt Olive (maniac)
Spears a bun and fires back.
When it hits one of the twins,
That's when Whirl War III begins.
Tickled sillies pitch their food,
Family members come unglued.
Then what happens? Happiness
I cannot fully express
When Grandpa in his gooey shirt,
Yells "Anybody for dessert?"

# Ballad of the Potato

What kind of dish are you serving up, Spud,
Now that you're no longer stuck in the mud?

> *I keep my eyes peeled for gardeners like you.*
> *I'd die for a casserole, soup, or beef stew.*

Oh, you are mouthwatering goodness, my Sweet,
Where butter, brown sugar, and marshmallows meet.

> *I've always been like this, I am what I am;*
> *How painful when someone mistakes me for Yam.*

Explain yourself, Frenchie, no one's ever seen
A snack quite as greasy or quicker cuisine.

> *If you've finished eating your burger and bun,*
> *Then roll me in catsup. I'm fast food and fun!*

Mix mustard and mayo in several of you
With celery, dill, onion, pepper (achoo!) . . .

> *It took you forever to see what's in store—*
> *Potatoes in salads! What ballads are for.*

National Potato Day

# Sweeeeet!

This fellow isn't hard to find
Inside a grocery store.
He's pouring maple syrup over
Words in Aisle 4.

Hug A Greeting Card Writer Day

# Our Invisible Friends

Run off to bed, dear chromosomes,
you've done it! Thanks to you,
some newborn's eyes have turned
amazing hazel, brown, or blue.
That brilliant map you gave the genes
told them about her eyes,
the color that her hair should be,
her shoe size, her hat size,
whether she will be right-handed,
wear a dainty nose,
and whether she will lean to liking
poetry or prose.
A ballet dancer? Pigeon-toed?
We'll have to wait and see.
For now, my little chromosomes,
you wrote biology.

National
DNA Day

# When Should We Meat?

If vegetarians have trouble
Finding tasty lip-smackers,
Aren't they allowed to cheat a bit
By eating animal crackers?

World
Vegetarian
Day

# Advice to the Young

How blissfully happy I was in those years
    When horses pulled carriages, son.
But someone has planted white hairs in my ears.
    Whoever said tweezers were fun?

My face may remind you of deep pitted prunes
    Or wrinkly waves on the sea.
I frightened a bear once, a skunk, two raccoons—
    My scarecrow's a picture of . . . *ME?!*

I wake up each morning for breakfast and pills
    To clear the cobwebs from my head,
Take a shower, feed the cat, read a poem, pay the bills . . .
    And then I am ready for bed.

My advice? You may think growing up will be great—
    You won't have to do what you're told.
But so many things you anticipate
    You won't want to do when you're old.

# Bluffing

A gambler who cheated at poker
Was exceptionally mediocre.
He said, "Bluffing's not hard.
After all, I'm a card!"
And the players just stared at the joker.

National Card Playing Day

# Vinegrrrrr

It was such a lovely day
   Till I stumbled in the way
Of a van that carries vinegar to stores.

   When I glared up at the man,
   Operator of the van,
He said, "Vinegar, it never rains but pours!"

   Now a skunk was standing by.
   And I thought that I might cry
For the vinegar completely soaked my clothes,

   Till the driver rudely yells,
   "Watch that animal. It smells!"—
And the skunk ran off, a hankie to her nose.

National
Vinegar Day

# Outhouses

World Toilet Day

I think that I shall never see
An outhouse lovely as a tree,
That ugly seat and what's below . . .
Unless I *really* have to go.

## For a Dentist

Plan Your Epitaph Day

I married a gal
Named Toothless Sal
She buried me
In a root canal

National Sportsmanship Day

# Tic-Tac-Toad

A Turkey and a Toad were playing
    Tic-tac-toe in Texas.
The Turkey said, "I'll take the O's,
    And you can have the X's."

But Armadillo scratched the game
    That Turtle cleaned and dusted,
Which made the Toad and Turkey tic-
    Tac-totally disgusted.